THE CUBAN MISSILE CRISIS

To the Brink of War

by Paul J. Byrne

THE CUBAN MISSILE CRISIS

To the Brink of War

by Paul J. Byrne

Content Adviser: Derek Shouba, Adjunct History Professor
and Assistant Provost, Roosevelt University

Reading Adviser: Susan Kesselring, M.A., Literacy Educator,
Rosemount–Apple Valley–Eagan (Minnesota) School District

COMPASS POINT BOOKS
MINNEAPOLIS, MINNESOTA

COMPASS POINT BOOKS

3109 West 50th Street, #115
Minneapolis, MN 55410

Visit Compass Point Books on the Internet at
www.compasspointbooks.com
or e-mail your request to
custserv@compasspointbooks.com

For Compass Point Books
Jennifer VanVoorst, Jaime Martens, XNR Productions, Inc.,
Catherine Neitge, Keith Griffin, and Carol Jones

Produced by White-Thomson Publishing Ltd.
Tel.: 0044 (0)1273 403990
210 High Street, Lewes BN7 2NH

For White-Thomson Publishing
Stephen White-Thomson, Brian Krumm, Amy Sparks, Tinstar Design
Ltd. *www.tinstar.co.uk*, Derek Shouba, Joselito F. Seldera, Bill Hurd,
and Timothy Griffin

Library of Congress Cataloging-in-Publication Data
Byrne, Paul J.
  The Cuban Missile Crisis : to the brink of war / by Paul J. Byrne.
  p. cm. — (Snapshots in history)
  Includes bibliographical references and index.
  ISBN 0-7565-1624-2 (hardcover)
  1. Cuban Missile Crisis, 1962—Juvenile literature. I. Title. II. Series.
  E841.B97 2006
  973.922—dc22   2005027153

WE BLOCKADE CUBA WITH 40 WARSHIPS
EL DIARIO
BLOQUEO A CASTRO

CONTENTS

World on the Brink

American President John F. Kennedy woke up to some alarming news on the morning of Tuesday, October 16, 1962. The 45-year-old president was sitting on the edge of his bed in the White House, reading the morning newspapers in his pajamas. His national security adviser, McGeorge Bundy, brought him the news he did not want to hear.

Bundy told President Kennedy that the U.S. government was in possession of photographs taken just the day before by a high-flying American U-2 spy plane. The photographs showed that the Soviet Union was secretly positioning ballistic missiles in Cuba, just 90 miles (145 kilometers) off the coast of Florida. For Kennedy and others in the U.S. government, their worst fears had come true.

When the crisis began, Kennedy had already spent a lot of time thinking about the relationship between the United States and the Soviet Union.

The president already had a lot on his mind in the fall of 1962. He had been busy traveling around the country on the campaign trail to support members of his political party in the upcoming November elections. Outside Washington, D.C., most Americans were focused on baseball's World Series between the New York Yankees and the San Francisco Giants. But in the back of everyone's minds, and especially people in Washington, was the ongoing conflict between the United States and Soviet Union, officially known as the Union of Soviet Socialist Republics (U.S.S.R.).

The United States and the Soviet Union had worked together to defeat Nazi Germany in World War II. But since the end of the war in 1945, they

Flying at altitudes of 70,000 feet (22,000 meters), the U-2 spy plane took highly detailed photographs of areas in Cuba and other countries.

had become fierce enemies. They had been waging a war of words and ideas. They competed with each other for allies and power around the world. They competed for territory, they competed at sea, and they even competed in space.

Both the United States and the U.S.S.R. built up military forces. In addition to their huge forces of aircraft, ships, tanks, and soldiers, both also had arsenals of thermonuclear weapons—hydrogen bombs. Each bomb was capable of destroying an entire city and killing millions of people in an instant. This real danger of complete destruction prevented either side from actually attacking the other. But that certainly did not stop the two sides from making threats.

This long era, which lasted from the end of World War II until the early 1990s, became known as the Cold War. It was called this because it was marked by a cold rivalry and small-scale confrontations around the world, as opposed to the "heat" of a full-scale war. On one side were the United States and most democracies in Western Europe, which were allied in the North Atlantic Treaty Organization (NATO). On the other side were the countries of the Warsaw Pact, an alliance of the U.S.S.R. and the communist nations of Eastern Europe.

The Soviet leader, Nikita S. Khrushchev, had been battling with U.S. President Dwight D. Eisenhower for years before Kennedy was elected. When the two leaders met in Vienna, Austria, in June 1961, Khrushchev got a chance to size up the young American president. Kennedy seemed to be at least a little intimidated by the older, more experienced Khrushchev, and Khrushchev might have thought he could push Kennedy around on the world stage.

KHRUSHCHEV

Nikita Sergeyevich Khrushchev was born to Ukrainian peasants in 1894. He joined the Communist Party in 1918 and soon rose through the ranks. He saw front-line action against the Germans in World War II. Khrushchev became leader of the Soviet Union soon after the death of the dictator Josef Stalin in 1953. His time as Soviet premier marked the most intense years of the Cold War.

The primary source of conflict between the two leaders was the divided city of Berlin, Germany, where Soviet and American military forces stood face to face. Germany itself was divided into West Germany, which was allied with NATO, and East Germany, which was allied with the U.S.S.R. in the Warsaw Pact.

Just a few months after the Kennedy-Khrushchev meeting in Vienna, the Soviets began building the Berlin Wall. This concrete wall would stand for almost three decades as a symbol of the Cold War, as well as a real, physical dividing line between East and West. If the two great powers were ever going to go to war, it might be for control of Berlin. But that scenario never developed. The Soviet missiles in Cuba started an entirely new crisis.

At their 1961 meeting in Vienna, Austria, President Kennedy (right) and Premier Khrushchev talked about the dangerous situation in Berlin, Germany, and about the real possibility of war between the United States and the Soviet Union.

President Kennedy was already certain that the Soviets were shipping weapons to Cuba. He and his military experts had figured these were non-nuclear arms meant only to defend Cuba. But there were rumors and reports of missiles on the island that could carry nuclear warheads and directly threaten the United States itself. The photos shown to President Kennedy on that Tuesday in October proved that the rumors of the missiles were true.

Missile trailers, launchers, and other equipment were visible from about 13 miles (21 km) above Cuba.

MRBM FIELD LAUNCH SITE
SAN CRISTOBAL NO 1
14 OCTOBER 1962

ERECTOR/LAUNCHER EQUIPMENT

TENT AREAS

EQUIPMENT

ERECTOR/LAUNCHER EQUIPMENT

8 MISSILE TRAILERS

14

Just six weeks earlier, the president had told the United States and the world that if there were Soviet offensive weapons in Cuba, "the gravest issues would arise." And speaking of a Cuban or Soviet threat against the United States or any other country in the Western Hemisphere, President Kennedy warned:

It will be prevented by whatever means necessary.

After seeing the U-2 photos, President Kennedy knew he had to do something. The question now was what to do—and how soon to do it.

At that very moment, just over 1,100 miles (1,770 km) to the south of Washington, D.C., the missiles in question were being prepared for battle by Soviet crews and their Cuban allies. If these missiles became operational, they could destroy American cities within minutes of being launched. Even Washington, D.C., itself was threatened. The Cold War that had always seemed far away, in other parts of the world, was now in America's own backyard. ◼

Communism Close to Home

Chapter

2

Cuba had not always been such a problem for the United States. The two countries had economic ties since the days of colonial America, and this relationship grew stronger through the years. Cuba had been a Spanish colony since the European settlement of the New World. Throughout the 19th century, Spain's influence in the Western Hemisphere grew weaker as the power and influence of the United States grew stronger. This led to conflict between Spain and the United States. The two countries went to war in 1898, mainly over control of Cuba—the largest, most economically important island in the Caribbean Sea.

The Spanish-American War marked the rise to world power of the United States. During this period, known as the Imperial Age, the United

Troops mounted on horseback fought in the Spanish-American War, a battle between Spain and the United States for control of Cuba.

States and other countries openly interfered in the affairs of other countries. After the Spanish-American War, the victorious Americans inserted what was known as the Platt Amendment into the new Cuban constitution. This amendment gave the United States the legal right to intervene in Cuban affairs. President Theodore Roosevelt even claimed the right of the United States to intervene in the affairs of any country in the Western Hemisphere if and when these countries "misbehaved."

Cuban workers helped cultivate sugarcane, a crop on which the economy of Cuba was dependent.

American businessmen invested a great deal of money in Cuba. Through their investments in Cuba, American corporations came to control

much of the Cuban economy, which was mostly based on the sugarcane industry. By the 1950s, Cuba seemed to have the highest standard of living in all of Latin America. Havana, the capital city, had become a popular destination for Americans to visit. However, not everyone saw the United States' role in Cuba as a positive thing for Cuba and its people. Many Cubans did not enjoy the high standards of living that U.S. involvement in the country seemed to promise. Many saw U.S. influence in their country as a source of corruption and injustice.

Fidel Castro was one of those Cubans. After college, he worked as a lawyer and soon became a popular revolutionary leader. When he was 32 years old, Castro led a small band of rebels to victory in the Cuban Revolution. The feared and hated dictator, Fulgencio Batista, who had been supported by the United States, fled the country on New Year's Day 1959. This allowed Castro and his followers to take power in the country. When the rebel army marched into Havana, people lined the streets to greet them as heroes.

THE REVOLUTIONARY

Fidel Castro was born in 1926. He had revolutionary ideas at an early age and helped organize a strike by sugar workers on his father's plantation when he was just 13 years old. He attended the best schools in Cuba and was such a rebellious student that he earned the nickname El Loco, or the "crazy one." He grew into an intelligent young man with big ideas. When he came to power in 1959, he was a hero to millions of people all over the world.

19

Fidel Castro (with arm raised) arrived in Havana soon after the former dictator fled Cuba.

Even before his revolutionary victory, Castro realized that, if he wanted to achieve his goals for this country, he would soon have to deal with

powerful Americans, who wanted to keep things as they were in Cuba:

> *Once this struggle is finished, I'll begin the real struggle of my life ... the fight I will wage against the United States. I believe that is my true destiny.*

At first, the new Cuban leader was accepted by the Americans and President Dwight Eisenhower, who had seen dictators come and go throughout Latin America. But Castro soon started taking actions that angered people in the United States, such as taking over American-owned properties and businesses.

U.S. HISTORY WITH CUBA	
1898	*Cuba granted independence after the United States defeats Spain in the Spanish-American War.*
1903	*Platt Amendment gives the United States the right to intervene in Cuban affairs.*
1906	*U.S. Marines occupy Cuba during civil unrest.*
1912	*U.S. Marines worked in Cuba to quell a rebellion by sugar workers.*
1917	*U.S. Marines intervene in Cuba, to secure sugar exports during World War I.*
1933	*American warships sent to Cuba; Fulgencio Batista takes over and is backed by the United States.*

As his relationship with the United States got worse, Castro's relations with the U.S.S.R. improved. When the United States refused to buy sugar from Cuba, which was very important to the Cuban economy, the Soviets agreed to buy the sugar. Cuba's ties to the U.S.S.R. were strengthened by two of Castro's closest advisers—his brother, Raul Castro, and the legendary revolutionary, Che Guevara. Both men shared the communist ideology of the Soviets. Castro himself had been careful not to appear too close to the Soviets. Behaving in this manner might have provoked a U.S. invasion. But Castro came to believe that the Americans would invade Cuba no matter what. This fear drove him into the arms of the Soviets. Soon the U.S.S.R. and its allies were providing military aid and weapons to Cuba.

A low-flying American jet photographed evidence of Soviet arms in Cuba.

MISSILE ERECTOR

CABLE

MISSILE SHELTER TENT

TRACKED PRIME MOVERS

OXIDIZER TANK TRAILERS

FUEL TANK TRAILERS

A happy Nikita Khrushchev gave Castro a huge bear hug when the two leaders met in New York in 1960.

Khrushchev and the Soviets couldn't have asked for a better-located ally against the United States. The Americans had allies all over the Eastern Hemisphere, surrounding the U.S.S.R. The United States had a huge number of military forces in Europe near Soviet borders, as well as forces in Japan and South Korea to Russia's east. To the south, Iran and Turkey, both U.S. allies, actually bordered the U.S.S.R. Turkey was a member of NATO. It was well known that the United States had nuclear missiles in Turkey, which were pointed at the Soviet Union.

THE CUBAN MISSILE CRISIS

Fidel Castro spoke to Cuban troops before an invasion by anti-Castro troops.

While the United States had forces surrounding the U.S.S.R., the Soviets had no military presence at all in the Western Hemisphere. They did not even

have aircraft carriers to put their planes within striking distance of the U.S. mainland. But the new alliance between Cuba and the U.S.S.R. changed all that, giving Khrushchev and the Soviets a military base less than 100 miles (161 km) from the United States. After the Soviets moved missiles to Cuba, the global balance of power would shift. That was something the U.S. government would not allow.

By the time John F. Kennedy became president at the beginning of 1961, the Americans were already working on ways to get rid of Fidel Castro. The U.S. government trained and armed anti-Castro Cubans, hoping that they would overthrow the dictator. This plan ended in a disaster with a failed invasion at the Bay of Pigs in April 1961. Castro and his men quickly defeated the ragtag army of 1,500 invaders, and the failure was a huge embarrassment for the Kennedy administration. Another failure early in Kennedy's presidency was a secret plan to assassinate Fidel Castro, known as Operation Mongoose. As much as they tried, the Americans just couldn't seem to get rid of Castro. Their failed schemes only helped to solidify Castro's alliance with the U.S.S.R.

OPERATION MONGOOSE

Operation Mongoose was the codename given to a plan by the U.S. government to assassinate Fidel Castro. The secret operation included a number of bizarre plans to kill the Cuban leader. Castro was known to smoke cigars, so exploding cigars were considered. The U.S. government also hatched a different scheme to lace Castro's food with chemicals that would make his facial hair fall out. U.S. leaders hoped that this might somehow make Castro less popular and even cause him to lose power.

The President's Men

Chapter

3

Back in Washington, D.C., President Kennedy and his advisers were debating what to do about the missiles in Cuba. On Tuesday, October 16, the same morning he learned about the photos, the president immediately called for a meeting. Kennedy and his advisers gathered before noon in the White House Cabinet Room.

Joining the president in the large room were several intelligence officers, who presented the photos and pointed out details showing the missiles. They were found in the area around San Cristobal, located in western Cuba. The president and his advisers pored over the evidence, asking the intelligence officers questions about the photos and the missiles. They wondered if there may have been more missiles in Cuba not seen in these spy photos.

President Kennedy had some initial discussions outside the White House with certain individuals, including Secretary of Defense Robert McNamara.

Along with key members of his Cabinet, the president assembled a team of experts to help him determine what to do. Most of these advisers were from the president's administration, but Kennedy also sought the advice of people outside his government who were experts on Soviet relations. This group became known as the Executive Committee of the National Security Council, or "EXCOMM" for short. Before the crisis was over, Kennedy would also seek the wisdom of former president Dwight Eisenhower, the much-respected World War II general who had led Americans through war and peace. The young president knew he needed all the advice he could get.

During the crisis, President Kennedy sought the advice of many people, including former president Dwight Eisenhower.

EXECUTIVE COMMITTEE OF THE NATIONAL SECURITY COUNCIL MEMBERS

Robert S. McNamara ....*Secretary of Defense*

Douglas Dillon ....*Secretary of the Treasury*

Dean Rusk ....*Secretary of State*

Ted Sorenson ....*White House Council*

Robert Kennedy......................................*Attorney General*

Alexis Johnson...........................*Deputy Secretary of State*

Lyndon Johnson ....*Vice President*

Edward Martin........................*Assistant Secretary of State*

McGeorge Bundy.......................*National Security Adviser*

Llewellyn Thompson ....*Former Ambassador to the U.S.S.R.*

John McCone ....*Central Intelligence Agency Director*

Roswell Gilpatric ....*Deputy Secretary of Defense*

George Ball ....*Undersecretary of State*

Paul Nitze ....*Assistant Secretary of Defense*

Maxwell Taylor..........*Chairman of the Joint Chiefs of Staff*

Kenneth O'Donnell......................................*White House Appointment Secretary*

Adlai Stevenson...................................*U.S. Ambassador to the United Nations*

Dean Acheson............................*Former Secretary of State*

Kennedy's Cabinet included some of the brightest minds of the day, drawn from different areas of American society. The Cabinet included business leaders and scholars as well as career politicians.

Robert Kennedy (left), the president's younger brother, was the U.S. attorney general.

Some of the Cabinet members had actually heard about the Soviet missiles in Cuba before the president himself. National Security Adviser McGeorge Bundy had decided to give the president

a good night's sleep before telling him about the missiles on Tuesday morning, which was probably a good idea since no one would be getting much sleep for the next few weeks.

The EXCOMM group met again later on Tuesday and every day over the following two weeks as the crisis deepened. The president tried to keep his regular schedule to avoid causing suspicion among Washington news reporters. The EXCOMM team did not want to draw attention with a convoy of government cars showing up at the White House, so for one meeting, nine of them piled into Robert Kennedy's car. Three sat in the front seat with the driver, and six crowded in the back seat. They entered the White House through a secret entrance known only to a select few.

PEARL HARBOR

President Kennedy and his advisers still had the surprise Japanese attack on Pearl Harbor in 1941 fresh in their minds. Kennedy and EXCOMM realized that the missiles in Cuba could be used in a similar surprise attack on the United States. The attack on Pearl Harbor ended up being devastating for Japan, just as a nuclear attack from Cuba would have been equally as devastating for Cuba and the Soviet Union. But EXCOMM wondered whether this kind of logic would stop Khrushchev from actually using the missiles.

Throughout the crisis, the president and top advisers encouraged everyone at the EXCOMM meetings to speak their minds. Normally, a person's rank is very important in the presidential chain of command and in executive decision-making, but it was more important to the president that he heard from everyone so that all options were explored.

31

At first, almost everyone thought the missiles should be destroyed with a bombing raid. Most wanted to strike without warning—it seemed like the only logical thing to do. The only question was what to do after the missile sites were bombed. Soviet warplanes in Cuba could threaten Florida or other southeastern U.S. locations. Should these aircraft and other targets in Cuba be bombed to prevent military retaliation? Should these bombing raids be followed by a full invasion of Cuba?

The more they talked, the more questions they asked themselves. The EXCOMM team started considering the consequences of any actions they might order. If they ordered an action without

President Kennedy secretly tape-recorded the EXCOMM meetings at the White House.

thinking it through, they could have a nuclear war on their hands.

Undersecretary of State George Ball was one of the few to speak out against a surprise attack. He was thinking about what would happen as a result of the attacks and what the Soviets would do in response. He told his fellow EXCOMM members his thoughts, saying:

This isn't the end. This is the beginning.

Ball was also worried about how such an attack would appear to the rest of the world, who at this point were unaware of the missiles.

33

He told the president:

Undersecretary of State George Ball was one of the first EXCOMM members to advise against air strikes.

> *It's the kind of conduct that one might expect from the Soviet Union. [But it is] not conduct that one expects from the United States.*

Attorney General Robert Kennedy, the president's brother and trusted adviser, began to see Ball's point of view. "George Ball has a good point," he said. Then he asked the other EXCOMM members:

> *Even if we survive ... what kind of country are we?*

Secretary of Defense Robert McNamara was the most businesslike person in EXCOMM. McNamara was a former chief executive officer (CEO) of Ford Motor Company. He tried to manage the meetings and make sure all the options were clear. McNamara warned his colleagues:

> *I don't believe we have considered the consequences. ... I really think we need to think these problems through more than we have.*

McNamara turned against the idea of surprise air strikes and instead suggested a naval blockade of Cuba as a first step. Yet, as secretary of defense, he oversaw the detailed planning for air strikes and an invasion of Cuba in case the president made those decisions.

John McCone, director of the Central Intelligence Agency (CIA), called for immediate air strikes. McCone had been pressing the president for months to start U-2 flights over Cuba in order to see whether rumors about missiles there were true. His instincts had proved to be right.

Defense Secretary McNamara (right) symbolized what President Kennedy called a "new generation of Americans."

Maxwell Taylor, the chairman of the Joint Chiefs of Staff, was not opposed to air strikes, but he wanted to ensure that his orders were clear. He also wanted to make sure that he and his men, the actual military personnel who would be taking action, had enough time to plan their attacks.

He told the president:

> *The more time we've got, the better we can do it.*

National Security Adviser Bundy agreed that air strikes were necessary but believed the United States would need to invade Cuba and get rid of Castro as well. He said:

> *I don't know what [a] blockade is going to solve ... I'm convinced that Castro has to go.*

But like other EXCOMM members, Bundy changed his mind as the crisis wore on. Who could blame him? They were all intelligent people, but they were under a lot of pressure and forced to make decisions that could turn world history one way or another. If the United States attacked without warning and killed thousands of people, including hundreds of Soviet troops, what would be the outcome? President Kennedy and the members of EXCOMM had to give serious consideration to this issue.

HAWKS VS. DOVES

President Kennedy's advisers during the crisis were split into "hawks" and "doves." Hawks were those who favored a forceful military response. Doves looked for peaceful, political solutions. These terms were used during the crisis, and the distinction is still referred to today.

The Loneliest Job in the World

Chapter

4

Though the EXCOMM debates continued, everyone knew it was going to be up to President Kennedy alone to make the decision. It could not have been an easy decision to make. No matter what action the president decided to take, there was a real danger of it leading to a nuclear war. Kennedy not only had to think about how the Soviets might react to American actions. He also had to think about how the American public would react, how the world would react, and how his decisions would affect U.S. allies around the globe. There has probably never been a time when the fate of so many people depended on the decision of one man.

By Friday, October 19, the fourth day of the crisis, the situation seemed as uncertain as ever. The president had about half his people telling him to destroy the missiles as soon as possible,

U.S. Marines listened to Brigadier General W.R. Collins, the commander of Marine ground forces in Cuba, as he discussed the possibility of a ground invasion of Cuba. The U.S. military base at Guantanamo Bay, Cuba, was evacuated during the missile crisis.

while the other half was urging him to be cautious and suggesting a naval blockade of Cuba. That morning, he met with the Joint Chiefs of Staff, the top commanders in each branch of the military. Not surprisingly, the chiefs were unanimous in their call for immediate military action, without warning.

The commanders saw the missiles in Cuba as a clear and present danger to U.S. security. They suggested that anything less than air strikes would not only endanger the American people, but would harm U.S. military strategy around the world. Air Force Chief Curtis LeMay even told Kennedy that after all the strong public warnings he had given about Soviet weapons in Cuba, a blockade would be seen as a "weak response" by allies of the United States, by the rest of the world, and by the American people themselves. The general then said to his commander in chief:

MEETING WITH THE ENEMY

Presidents often meet with representatives of foreign nations. Kennedy's schedule for October 18 happened to include a meeting with Andrei Gromyko, the Soviet foreign minister. When Kennedy asked about offensive Soviet weapons in Cuba, Gromyko told him that there were none. After the meeting, Kennedy told some of his advisers that Gromyko had "told more lies than I have ever heard in so short a time."

> *You're in a pretty bad fix, Mr. President.*

The annoyed president glared at the general and asked, "What did you say?" After LeMay repeated what he had said, Kennedy reminded the general, "You are in it with me."

Even though the general may have been out of line, he was right; the president was indeed in a fix. But it came down to two choices: air strikes to eliminate the missiles, followed by an invasion of Cuba, or a naval blockade, which would stop all ships from bringing weapons to Cuba and leave open the possibility of a peaceful solution. Either way would be a direct use of military force, which could easily get out of control. And whether the president chose one or the other option, there would be some who questioned the decision.

President Kennedy met with Soviet diplomats Anatoly Dobrynin and Andrei Gromyko on October 18. He thought about confronting them with the spy photos but decided to keep them a secret.

The air strikes would have taken care of the immediate threat posed by the missiles, but there was really no telling what the Soviets would do. Even if the Soviets did nothing in Cuba in response to the air strikes, they could have attacked American allies in another part of the world—Turkey, where the United States had nuclear missile bases of its own, or NATO forces in West Berlin. Either way, the Americans would need to respond to any Soviet action, wherever in the world it might be, and the conflict could soon become World War III.

Kennedy had to be asking himself if it was worth it to lose West Berlin to the Soviets and to risk starting World War III over the missiles. After all, if the Soviets really wanted to start a war by bombing American cities, they had the missiles to do that in the Soviet Union itself. Both the Americans and the Soviets had intercontinental ballistic missiles (ICBMs) that could reach around the world.

Viewed this way, the missiles in Cuba did not change the strategic balance. It didn't matter if the missile came from Cuba or Siberia. As Secretary of Defense McNamara said:

A missile is a missile.

The president decided that a naval blockade of Cuba would allow Soviet Premier Khrushchev time to rethink what he was doing in Cuba, and unlike the air strike scenario, it would not force him to retaliate to protect the prestige of the Soviet Union.

But the naval blockade had its own set of risks and could easily result in all-out war if ships started getting sunk. It wasn't a perfect solution, but the president believed it was the best option he had.

Missiles launched from Cuba would be able to reach several major cities in the United States and Mexico.

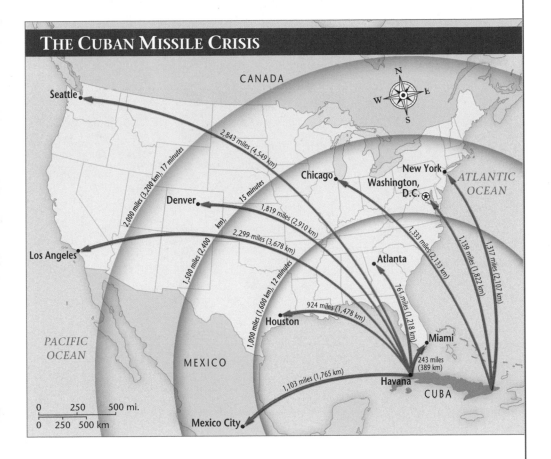

THE CUBAN MISSILE CRISIS

President Kennedy announced that he would speak to the people of the United States on the evening of October 22 about "a matter of highest national urgency." Kennedy and the members of EXCOMM spent the weekend notifying other government officials about the missiles and about what the United States was planning to do.

At the same time, they notified allies in Europe and around the world. Secretary of State Dean Rusk even shared an advance copy of the president's speech with the Soviet ambassador Anatoly Dobrynin. It included a personal note from Kennedy to Khrushchev, warning Khrushchev that he should not misjudge the willingness of the United States to act with more force if need be.

Shortly before he was to appear on television on Monday evening, President Kennedy held a tense hour-long meeting with members of Congress to explain the crisis and the actions he was about to take. Several senators demanded that the president take more forceful action, while others agreed to support the president's decision. The president left the meeting very frustrated and upset, telling his aide Ted Sorenson:

If they want the job they can have it.

But Kennedy then reminded himself that these senators had just learned about the missiles and were reacting emotionally. They did not have the week he and his advisers had to think through the consequences.

On the evening of Monday, October 22, televisions around the country were tuned to the president's speech. At the time, there were only a few television networks, and each broadcast the speech. Despite leaving the tense meeting with Congress just an hour before, and having spent a week of endless debates and sleepless nights, the president appeared relaxed and confident as he spoke to the nation at 7:00 P.M.

Kennedy calmly explained the crisis to the American people. The following are some highlights from his speech:

> *Good evening my fellow citizens. This government, as promised, has maintained the closest surveillance of the Soviet military buildup on the island of Cuba. Within the past week, unmistakable evidence has established the fact that a series of offensive*

In his speech, Kennedy promised a "full retaliatory response" against the Soviet Union if any missile was launched from Cuba to the United States.

missile sites is now in preparation on that imprisoned island. The purpose of these bases can be none other than to provide a nuclear strike capability against the Western Hemisphere.

Cuban exiles, who had fled to the United States when Castro took over in Cuba, watched intently as the president gave his famous speech.

This secret, swift, and extraordinary buildup of communist missiles ... cannot be accepted by this country, if our courage and our commitments are ever to be trusted again by either friend or foe.

> *Our policy has been one of patience and restraint, as befits a peaceful and powerful nation, which leads a worldwide alliance. But now further action is required—and it is under way; and these actions may only be the beginning. We will not prematurely or unnecessarily risk the costs of worldwide nuclear war in which even the fruits of victory would be ashes in our mouth—but neither will we shrink from that risk at any time it must be faced.*

> *I call upon Chairman Khrushchev to halt and eliminate this clandestine, reckless, and provocative threat to world peace and to stable relations between our two nations. I call upon him further to abandon this course of world domination, and to join in an historic effort to end the perilous arms race and to transform the history of man.*

In a speech that lasted nearly 20 minutes, he told his fellow citizens about the missiles and how they were discovered. He explained the different kinds of missiles, the distances they could travel, and what they were capable of doing. He reminded Americans of the recent statements and warnings he had made and how the Soviets had made false statements. He went on to say that the United States could not tolerate this "provocative and unjustified change in the status quo," and then he laid out the steps the government was already taking to deal with the threat.

47

The Courtroom of World Opinion

Chapter

5

At the United Nations (U.N.) headquarters in New York City, U.S. Ambassador to the United Nations Adlai Stevenson requested an urgent meeting of the U.N. Security Council to deal with this threat to world peace. Stevenson delivered his request immediately following the president's speech to the nation. At the time of the crisis, Valerian Zorin, the Soviet ambassador to the United Nations, happened to be the serving president of the council. With the Soviet ambassador getting the message directly from the Americans, the debate at the United Nations was off to a quick start.

The American ambassador called for the U.N. Security Council to make immediate demands for the Soviets to dismantle the missiles. Stevenson knew, however, that any resolution

The president normally used ceremonial pens when signing proclamations or other important documents; the pens would then be given out as gifts. When he signed the quarantine proclamation, however, Kennedy used only one pen to sign his name. This was strictly business.

The day after the president's speech, headlines around the world focused on the threat of war.

like this from the Security Council would be vetoed by the U.S.S.R., one of the five permanent members of the U.N. Security Council. These five members could veto any Security Council resolution. Ambassadors Stevenson and Zorin would soon meet again to battle it out at the United Nations.

Around the world, people were alarmed and frightened by the news. Tuesday morning's newspaper headlines presented the crisis as a showdown between President Kennedy and Premier Khrushchev.

A majority of Americans supported their president, but many feared the crisis could turn into a disaster. Kennedy was also supported by America's allies in Europe, even though they were nervous about the risks being taken by the American president.

Many newspapers and reporters in Great Britain, the closest ally of the United States, and elsewhere in the world responded with alarm. They called the blockade an act of war and criticized the president for causing this world crisis. Some critics even questioned whether the president's speech was meant to help his political party in the upcoming elections.

ORGANIZATION OF AMERICAN STATES

The Organization of American States (OAS) is one of the oldest international organizations in the world. It was formed in 1948, and came out of the earlier Pan-American Union. Kennedy's government received the full support of the OAS during the missile crisis. This must have surprised Kennedy and Khrushchev, because the OAS was usually not so united. Cuba is a member of the OAS but it was suspended from taking part in the organization before the crisis began and was still suspended as of 2005.

Even though President Kennedy and his men believed their actions were justified, a great many people in the world thought that the Americans were equally to blame for the crisis. Only the EXCOMM members and a few others had seen the U-2 photos. The United States still had not shown the world any evidence of the missiles since President Kennedy's dramatic speech.

51

Many in the world thought the United States was being the aggressor and held it responsible for bringing the world to the brink of nuclear war.

Many neutral nations did not share the American view of Cuba. Castro and his revolution were very popular in places around the world. After the American role in the failed Bay of Pigs invasion of Cuba, the international community had good reason to be suspicious of the United States announcing this crisis to the world.

The U.N. representative from the African nation of Ghana said what many in Africa and Asia felt—that the United States and U.S.S.R. were both "rascals." Even if the Soviets were placing missiles in Cuba, it seemed to much of the world that the missiles were there to defend Cuba against the United States—just as U.S. missiles in Turkey were supposed to be there only to defend its allies against the Soviet Union.

Khrushchev angrily rejected the American blockade, calling it piracy on the high seas and threatening that the Soviets would protect their rights by force if need be. He said that Soviet ships would not obey the U.S. quarantine and, along with Castro, denounced the blockade as "Yankee imperialism."

The stage was set for a showdown in the U.N. Security Council. The Security Council chamber at the United Nations was filled with tension, but it was the perfect public setting for the United States and U.S.S.R. to present their cases to the world.

With more than 100 seats reserved for press reporters and additional seating for the public, Security Council diplomats sat in the middle of the room under bright lights. They were literally on the center stage of world relations.

Adlai Stevenson was the U.S. ambassador to the United Nations at the time of the crisis.

UNITED STATES

53

The chamber was much more crowded than usual, and people were milling around anxiously, trying to keep up with the ongoing debate between the American ambassador, Adlai Stevenson, and the Soviet ambassador, Valerian Zorin.

Stevenson and Zorin sat face to face, only six seats away from one another at a semicircular table. Stevenson was growing frustrated with Zorin's refusal to admit there were Soviet missiles in Cuba. The American ambassador directed his question at the Soviet representative:

> *All right, sir, let me ask you one simple question. Do you, Ambassador Zorin, deny that the U.S.S.R. has placed and is placing medium- and intermediate-range missiles and sites in Cuba? Yes or no?*

And then, breaking all diplomatic rules of engagement, Stevenson quickly added, "Don't wait for the translation, yes or no?" "I am not in an American courtroom, sir," Zorin blasted back at him.

The Soviet ambassador said he would not answer questions as if from a prosecutor:

> *In due course, sir, you will have your answer.*

Stevenson skillfully reminded Zorin:

> *You are in the courtroom of world opinion right now and you can answer yes or no.*

After the flustered Zorin still refused to answer the question, Stevenson told him:

> *I am prepared to wait for my answer until hell freezes over.*

Soviet ambassador Valerian Zorin (left) was surprised by U-2 surveillance shots of Soviet weapons and equipment in Cuba.

The U-2 surveillance photos Stevenson displayed offered evidence to support his claims.

The diplomats and others in the council chamber stood there with their mouths open. They were shocked by Stevenson's blunt words. Such an exchange had rarely if ever been heard before by the Security Council. And then the veteran diplomat had one more trick up his sleeve. Stevenson told Zorin and everyone else:

> *I am also prepared to present evidence in this room.*

He then turned everyone's attention directly behind him as his assistants uncovered large easels, containing photographs that had been hidden while the debate was going on. These were the same U-2 photographs President Kennedy had seen showing the missile sites in Cuba, and they had until now been seen only by people in the U.S. government. Stevenson was displaying the photos for the whole world to see, and it was the first time most people were seeing the evidence.

The episode was one of the most memorable moments ever experienced at the United Nations, and it convinced many people in the world that the Americans were telling the truth. But Khrushchev and the Soviets already knew the truth, and they were not backing down. ◣

Days of Uncertainty

Chapter

6

Hundreds of miles off the eastern coast of Florida, the U.S. Navy had set up a quarantine line in a huge arc from northern Florida to Puerto Rico. It extended 500 miles (805 km) from the easternmost tip of Cuba and engulfed all the northern Caribbean Sea. The line was focused to the north because this was the direction from which ships from the Soviet Union and Europe would be coming. It was where the Atlantic Ocean meets the Caribbean Sea, and these international waters were now filled with U.S. Navy vessels. President Kennedy signed a quarantine proclamation on Tuesday, October 23, putting the blockade into effect the next day, Wednesday, at 10:00 A.M.

As ships bound for Cuba approached the quarantine line, no one was sure what would happen. Khrushchev had warned that his Soviet ships would not turn back, and that he would have his submarines sink American ships if they interfered with Soviet vessels on their way to Cuba.

The Americans knew where the approaching ships were in the Atlantic Ocean from radar and surveillance planes, and they had plotted the courses of ships suspected of carrying missiles or other weapons. They also knew that at least six Soviet submarines were in the area. It was only a matter of time until the U.S. Navy would confront these ships.

The U.S. Army set up anti-aircraft missiles on beaches in Key West, Florida, and other places to protect against a possible attack by Soviet warplanes based in Cuba, only 90 miles (145 km) away.

Kennedy and Khrushchev corresponded back and forth during these most intense days of the crisis. Khrushchev questioned why Kennedy had so publicly pushed the world to the brink of nuclear destruction. Kennedy kept insisting that the missiles would have to be removed from Cuba. He told Khrushchev that this was the only way to end the crisis.

EXCOMM was now meeting every morning, and the meetings grew increasingly intense as the crisis wore on. Defense Secretary McNamara presided over the blockade from the Pentagon. Kennedy himself stayed heavily involved as at least 20 Cuba-bound ships approached the quarantine line from the northeast.

The president and government officials at the White House had direct lines of communication with naval commanders as U.S. ships began coming into contact with the foreign vessels late on Wednesday morning. President Kennedy and other U.S. government officials feared that a Soviet submarine might try to

AMERICAN MOBILIZATION

During the crisis, the U.S. military was rapidly building up forces for war. Nuclear bombers were on full alert and in the air constantly, with a bomber taking off to replace every one that landed. Approximately 100,000 troops from the National Reserves were moved into Georgia and Florida for a possible invasion of Cuba. At sea, there were 180 Navy ships, including destroyers, cruisers, aircraft carriers, and several submarines, in the area. Dozens of support ships were also taking part in the blockade. Most of the naval force was in place by Monday, before the president's speech to the nation.

defend the incoming ships by taking action against American warships and that this would lead to a larger confrontation.

During the crisis, a poster in Brazil read, "Hail Kennedy, the Defender of the Americas."

SALVE KENNEDY

O DEFENSOR DAS AMERICAS

The tension eased, however, as reports came in that some of the Soviet ships were changing course to avoid crossing the quarantine line. More than half of the ships being monitored reversed course, including those suspected of having missiles and other weapons onboard.

Khrushchev must have given the order for these ships to alter course at the last minute. However, other ships kept steaming

A BROTHER'S THOUGHTS

Robert Kennedy remembered his older brother's growing nervousness as they monitored the approaching ships. The president's "hand went up to his face and covered his mouth. He opened and closed his fist. The president's face seemed drawn, his eyes pained." President Kennedy was worried about the potential consequences of the situation.

In one of the few direct confrontations at sea the USS J.R. Pierce (left), along with another destroyer, the USS Joseph P. Kennedy, stopped and boarded a Cuba-bound freighter on October 26. The USS Kennedy was named for the president's older brother, who had died a hero in World War II.

toward Cuba. These were civilian, not military, ships, but they were still expected to stop if intercepted by U.S. warships. Kennedy gave orders that the remaining ships be trailed but not stopped.

After the suspect ships had turned around, Secretary of State Rusk told the other EXCOMM members:

> *We're eyeball to eyeball and I think the other fella just blinked.*

But the truth was that Kennedy was blinking as well. He was determined to do whatever it took to avoid the outbreak of a full-scale war. And the danger was far from over.

63

It was not until the morning of Friday, October 26, that an offending ship was stopped and boarded as part of the blockade. President Kennedy specifically chose a non-Soviet ship. He did this to show that the United States would enforce the blockade, while not forcing Khrushchev to follow through on his threat to sink U.S. ships that interfered with Soviet ships. The ship was inspected by U.S. naval officers, found to have no weapons, and allowed to continue to Cuba.

However, in the early hours of Saturday morning, a U-2 aircraft flown by Major Rudolf Anderson, who had captured some of the first photographs of the missiles in Cuba on an earlier mission, was shot down over Cuba by Soviet-made surface-to-air missiles (SAMs). The plane was destroyed; the young pilot was dead.

The news of the downed U-2 was a huge blow to Kennedy and EXCOMM. They questioned whether it was Soviet troops, acting under Khrushchev, who were manning the SAM sites, or if it was renegade Cubans firing anti-aircraft missiles. Either way, it was clear to most that the United States would now have to retaliate against the SAM sites in Cuba. Most presidential advisers now argued that when the U.S. Air Force took out the SAM sites, they should take out the ballistic missile sites as well.

These were some of the most uncertain hours of the crisis. Kennedy and his advisers continued to prepare for the worst, even as they hoped for a

peaceful solution to the crisis. They could soon be ready to bomb the missile sites, invade Cuba, and risk the outbreak of World War III.

With missiles backing them up, Kennedy and his military leaders were ready to go to war at a moment's notice.

Before the crisis had begun, Kennedy had been reading the book *The Guns of August.* The book, published in 1962, described how European powers had stumbled into World War I. Like the Americans and the Soviets during the missile crisis, the powers in 1914 had their own set of military strategies, goals, and expectations. The European system of alliances and their previously made military plans seemed to force the powers into war. Certainly none of them expected the horrors of World War I. Kennedy was determined, especially in an age in which entire cities could be vaporized, not to repeat the mistakes of the past. ◣

65

The End of the World?

Chapter

7

As the debates went on within the White House, at the United Nations, and around the world, the U.S. military was in full gear. Americans watched as tens of thousands of troops and masses of military hardware continued moving into Florida and the southeast United States in preparation for a possible invasion of Cuba.

General Thomas Power of Strategic Air Command (SAC) moved the U.S. nuclear bomber fleet to full-war alert—DEFCON 2. This meant that 550 American B-52s were in the air on full alert, carrying nuclear bombs and ready to strike anywhere in the world at any time. General Power had raised the alert level without authorization from the Defense Secretary or the president, both his superiors in

A 10-megaton hydrogen bomb packed five times as much destruction as all the firepower used in World War II and could flatten a city in seconds. Test blasts around the Bikini Atoll area in the Pacific Ocean proved the H-bomb to be the most destructive weapon ever made.

the chain of command. He had also raised the alert "out of code," meaning that the Soviets were sure to intercept the message. The only reason for doing so was to frighten the Soviets.

President Kennedy was furious. He was doing everything he could to avoid a nuclear war, and the generals were acting behind his back. This led the president and his closest advisers to believe that the military leadership had its own agenda in the crisis and was determined to go to war. U.S. presidents have always had clear constitutional authority over the military in their role as commander in chief. During the crisis, it seemed that some top military commanders were challenging this authority.

The days of the crisis were the scariest many people had ever lived through. Grocery store shelves were swept clean, as people stocked up on food and other things needed to survive in case the bombs fell. Government civil-defense activities included daily air raid drills in schools and elsewhere, teaching children and adults how to "duck and cover" in case of a nuclear blast. There was also a spike in the bomb shelter business. Families could get a do-it-yourself shelter for as little as $30. Other models could cost from a few hundred dollars up to $5,000 for a deluxe model.

Every evening of the week after President Kennedy's speech, people watched Walter Cronkite, the legendary CBS anchorman and the voice of nightly news for generations of Americans. Audiences watched live coverage as the Soviet ships came to the quarantine line. Cronkite wondered along with his viewers what was going to happen out at sea, as the blockade continued. The threat of war seemed closer than ever.

Schoolchildren were prepared for nuclear attacks with bomb drills in which they used their desks for protection.

Protestors demonstrated in front of the White House against the threatened invasion of Cuba.

Charles Lion was in the U.S. Air Force at the time of the missile crisis. He remembered the experience he had immediately after hearing the president's speech:

> *We watched Kennedy's speech in the rec room and as soon as he finished the base siren went off. We all assumed that there was going to be a war, probably a nuclear war.*

Former New Jersey Senator Robert Torricelli remembered:

> *The Cuban Missile Crisis was one of the most vivid experiences in my life. Watching the television and waiting for the reports of whether the Russian freighter was going to reverse course. Going to the supermarket with my parents, and they carried that list from the newspaper of the things you needed to have in the basement if there was a nuclear war. Then my parents set up a battery radio and cots and sleeping bags in the basement, things to store water and a lot of canned food. I think some of it stayed there until we sold the house in 1986.*

During the crisis, many people went to bed wondering whether they would live to see the next sunrise. However, as scared as many people were as they watched the crisis unfold, most of them probably did not know just how close the world was to a nuclear nightmare.

BERT THE TURTLE

"Bert the Turtle" was the star of the civil defense cartoon *Duck and Cover*. The cartoon was created in 1950 and taught children how to quickly drop to the floor or ground and find cover in case of danger. The cartoon's jingle told American children that Bert was alert and never got hurt because when he saw danger he would duck and cover.

In the late hours between Friday night and Saturday morning, October 26 and 27, Fidel Castro wrote a letter for the Soviet ambassador to send on directly to Khrushchev.

In his letter, it appeared that Castro was telling Khrushchev that if Cuba needed to be sacrificed in the battle against the United States, then he and the Cuban people were ready to give up their lives to defeat imperialism and the United States.

Castro was convinced that a U.S. invasion was coming. He had mobilized about 300,000 Cuban troops and militiamen after Kennedy's speech. With this many Cuban soldiers, a Soviet force that numbered in the tens of thousands, and all the Soviet weapons in Cuba, invading U.S. forces would have faced a tough fight with very heavy casualties. The Americans did not know that Soviet troops based in Cuba had battlefield-ready nuclear weapons that could have been used against invading U.S. troops. If the American attack was ordered and the Soviet nuclear weapons were launched against the invasion force, a full-scale nuclear war might have been unavoidable. ◣

Castro's Cuban army placed anti-aircraft guns around Havana.

73

Saved from the Brink

Chapter

8

President Kennedy was now faced with yet another tough decision. After the U-2 was shot down early Saturday morning, military commanders were demanding that missile sites in Cuba be destroyed. Being a military veteran himself, Kennedy might have felt a desire to retaliate for the loss of the pilot and the downing of the plane, but as president, he had to think of the bigger picture. President Kennedy still would not order the attack on Cuba. He was determined to avoid the outbreak of war.

Khrushchev had sent a letter to Kennedy on Friday, October 26, that seemed to offer a way out of the crisis. The Soviet premier said again in his letter that his nation was only interested in protecting Cuba, but he offered to dismantle and remove the Soviet missiles in return for a pledge from Kennedy that the United States would not invade Cuba.

In the letter, Khrushchev spoke directly to Kennedy, saying:

> *If indeed war should break out, then it would not be in our power to stop it, for such is the logic of war.*

It was the first time in the crisis that Kennedy was hearing that Khrushchev was just as human as he and shared the same fears he had. In reading Khrushchev's letter, Kennedy must have known exactly how the Soviet premier felt.

A second letter from Khrushchev arrived the following day. In this second letter, the Soviets demanded not only a pledge not to invade Cuba, but also the removal of American missiles from Turkey. It was evident to the president and EXCOMM members that this letter was more in line with what more-militant Soviet officials were demanding.

President Kennedy could not publicly agree to remove the missiles, since this might be seen as the United States abandoning Turkey, its NATO ally, under threat from the U.S.S.R. But while EXCOMM was discussing the Soviets' offer, they received a secret message from Khrushchev. The

JUPITER MISSILES

The United States had placed missiles known as Jupiter missiles in Turkey in 1956. However, U.S. submarines in the region carried Polaris missiles that would offer more protection to the allies in the area. Kennedy wanted to remove the missiles in Turkey even before the crisis began, but they became a secret bargaining chip.

No. 8

UNOFFICIAL TRANSLATION OF
LETTER FROM PREMIER KHRUSHCHEV TO
PRESIDENT KENNEDY

October 27, 1962

Esteemed Mr. President:

I have learned with great pleasure of your reply to Mr. Thant to the effect that steps will be taken to exclude contact between our ships and thus avoid irremediable fateful consequences.

This reasonable step on your part strengthens my belief that you are showing concern to safeguard peace and I note this with satisfaction.

"I have already said that our people, our Government and I personally, as Chairman of the Council of Ministers, are concerned solely that our countries should develop and occupy a worthy place among all peoples of the world in economic competition, in the development of culture and the arts, in raising the well being of the people. This is the most noble and necessary field for competition and victors as well as vanquished will only gain from it because it means peace and increased commodities for the life and enjoyment of man.

In your statement you supported the opinion that the main aim was, not only to come to an agreement and to take measures to prevent contact between our ships, and therefore the deepening of the crisis which may as a result of such a contact strike the fire of a military conflict, after which all talks would be superfluous, because other forces and other laws would come into force, the laws of war.

I agree with you that this is only the first step. The main thing that must be done is to normalize and stabilize the state of peace among states, among peoples.

I understand your concern for the security of the U.S.A. Mr. President, because this is the first duty of a President. But we are worried about the same questions: and I bear the same obligations, as Chairman of the Council of Ministers of the USSR.

You have been worried concerning the fact that we have helped Cuba with weapons, with the aim to strengthen its defensive capacity — yes, precisely its "defensive capacity," because no matter what weapons it possesses, Cuba cannot equal you: because these are different quantities, all the more so if one takes into consideration the modern means of extermination.

Our aim

message said Khrushchev would accept the terms of his first letter, without the need for the United States to publicly remove the missiles in Turkey.

On Saturday night, Robert Kennedy personally delivered his brother's response to Khrushchev by visiting the Soviet ambassador, Anatoly Dobrynin. The attorney general told the ambassador that the United States would agree not to invade Cuba in return for the dismantling and removal of the Soviet missiles from Cuba under U.N. supervision.

He also let Dobrynin know that the United States had planned to remove the American missiles in Turkey anyway and that they would be removed within six months. But if the Soviets publicly claimed this as part of the deal, the United States would deny it.

Robert Kennedy stressed to the Soviet ambassador that time was running out. He told Dobrynin that the United States knew the ballistic missiles in Cuba were being prepared for battle-readiness. If the work on the missiles continued to make them ready for launch, or if another American plane was shot down, then the United States would be forced to attack. The attack could come within a day or even hours. This was the last chance for a peaceful, diplomatic solution to the crisis.

The next morning in Moscow, Khrushchev called a meeting of the Soviet Presidium, the leadership council of the U.S.S.R. He told his comrades:

In order to save the world, we must retreat.

Khrushchev then sent a letter to President Kennedy publicly accepting the diplomatic solution and agreeing to dismantle the missiles. It read in part:

The Soviet government ... has given a new order to dismantle the arms which you describe as offensive, and to crate and return them back to the Soviet Union.

American soldiers based in Germany were relieved to read about the end of the crisis in The Stars and Stripes.

Khrushchev had always thought that Kennedy and the Americans were too idealistic to fight. Now he had seen the tougher side of Kennedy. The U.S. president ordered his advisers and government officials not to claim publicly any sort of victory at the end of the crisis. Kennedy realized that the whole world, including the Soviets, had "won" by avoiding a nuclear disaster.

President Kennedy and Premier Khrushchev were two men who brought the world to the brink of nuclear war, but they were also the men who saved the world from nuclear war. Kennedy refused to follow the military "rules of engagement" that were given to him, which seemed to call for military solutions without consideration of the consequences and obeyed only the "logic of war" as Khrushchev called it.

President Kennedy forced himself and his advisers to see things from their enemy's point of view, and this helped them find a peaceful solution of the crisis. Kennedy realized that Khrushchev also had people pressuring him to act stronger and to use military force. As Defense Secretary McNamara later recalled:

> *In the Cuban missile crisis, at the end, I think we did put ourselves in the skin of the Soviets.*

With his personal letter to Kennedy, Khrushchev spoke to the president as a fellow human being. Although it seemed as if he backed down, Khrushchev also got at least some of what he wanted from the solution to the crisis—an American commitment to not invade Cuba and the eventual removal of U.S. missiles from Turkey.

In Cuba, however, Fidel Castro felt that Khrushchev had betrayed him. The crisis quietly lingered on into November, as Castro refused to cooperate with U.N. surveillance teams that were to confirm the removal of the missiles. American military forces remained mobilized for weeks, and the naval quarantine was not officially lifted until November 20, after Soviet ships carried the dismantled missiles off Cuba and back to the U.S.S.R.

A Time to Remember

Chapter

9

Fidel Castro had been certain that once the Soviet missiles were out of Cuba, the United States would go back on its promise and invade his country. But a U.S. invasion of Cuba never came. The missiles were originally placed in Cuba to prevent an American invasion. However, when the Americans discovered them, it was the presence of the missiles that almost caused the United States to invade.

But there was more to the Cuban Missile Crisis than most people knew. Eventually, it was discovered that the Soviets did not have nearly as many nuclear weapons as the United States at the time of the crisis. Khrushchev knew this, and he might have thought that putting missiles into Cuba, close to the United States, would strengthen his position in the world.

J.B.K.   J.F.K.

★ OCTOBER 1962 ★

SUN	MON	TUE	WED	THU	FRI	SAT
	1	2	3	4	5	6
7	8	9	10	11	12	13
14	15	16	17	18	19	20
21	22	23	24	25	26	27
28	29	30	31			

President Kennedy had memento calendars made to give to the advisers who worked with him during the crisis.

Khrushchev's interests were also closer to home—in Berlin. Even if the missiles in Cuba gave the Soviets no real military advantage, Khrushchev knew they would give him at least a psychological advantage in people's minds. He might have believed that he could use the missiles in Cuba to force the Americans to give up West Berlin, but that never happened.

President John F. Kennedy was assassinated a little more than a year after the crisis—on November 22, 1963, in Dallas, Texas. The assassin, Lee Harvey Oswald, was a communist and an open supporter of Fidel Castro's Cuba.

THE CUBAN MISSILE CRISIS

President Kennedy was assassinated about an hour after he arrived in Dallas, Texas, with his wife Jackie in November 1963.

Before he was killed, the president signed an important arms control treaty that helped ease tensions with the Soviets. The president also helped create a telephone hotline, a direct line of

communication between the American president and the Soviet premier that was used when dangerous situations arose. This was done so that these two most important men in the world could always talk directly to each other when needed, rather than relying on military or official diplomatic channels to speak for them in times of crisis.

Khrushchev was forced out of power in the Soviet Union in 1964, less than two years after the crisis. The main charge against him was that he mishandled the whole Cuban affair and damaged the Soviet Union's global military strategy.

In the late 1980s, the Cold War ended where it had begun 40 years earlier—in Berlin. The once powerful Soviet Union had lost its appetite for confrontation with the United States and its allies. In November 1989, the Berlin Wall came down, and the people of East and West Germany united in celebration. The Soviet Union collapsed just a few years later, and through the 1990s divided into a number of independent countries, including Russia, Ukraine, Kazakhstan, and others.

Both the United States and Russia still have thousands of nuclear weapons. Fortunately, there is no longer much danger of a full-scale nuclear war between these two countries.

FORTIETH ANNIVERSARY CONFERENCE

Some people involved in the crisis, including Castro and McNamara, gathered for an anniversary conference of the crisis in Havana in October 2002. Declassified information was shared and secrets revealed by the Americans, the Cubans, and former Soviets involved in the crisis.

However, the danger of nuclear weapons being developed and used by other countries, or falling into the hands of terrorist organizations, is as real as ever.

Today, the Cuban Missile Crisis is remembered as the closest the world has come to nuclear war. It also perfectly represents what the larger battle of the whole Cold War was all about. While they faced off against each other around the world, neither the U.S.S.R. nor the United States really wanted to fight each other in a full-scale war. Leaders in both countries came to realize that, with their horrible weapons, a war between them could have truly meant the end of the world. So instead of fighting each other with military

The fall of the Berlin Wall in November 1989 perfectly symbolized the end of the Cold War.

force, they mostly limited their war to ideological and psychological battles and supported allies in actual fighting around the world.

But it was during those two weeks in October 1962 when the danger of a nuclear holocaust was at its highest and the fear that it might actually happen was most intense. Secretary of State Dean Rusk had said that the Soviets "blinked." For 13 terrible days, neither side seemed ready to back down from the brink, and everyone involved was holding his breath. But in the end, the world was saved because everyone blinked. Everyone knew that a war in the nuclear age could only lead to global disaster. ▨

Timeline

January 1, 1959

Fidel Castro takes power in Cuba after Fulgencio Batista, the Cuban dictator, flees the country

September 1960

Shipments of weapons and other military equipment begin arriving in Cuba from Warsaw Pact countries

October 1960

Castro nationalizes more than 1 billion dollars worth of American property and investments in Cuba, meaning private property is taken without compensation; the United States responds by restricting all trade with Cuba

January 20, 1961

John F. Kennedy is inaugurated as the 35th U.S. president

April 1961

Cuban exiles backed by the U.S. Central Intelligence Agency attempt to overthrow Castro; their invasion fails and becomes known as the Bay of Pigs invasion

June 1961

Kennedy and Soviet Premier Nikita Khrushchev meet in Vienna, Austria

August 12, 1961

Construction begins on the Berlin Wall

November 1961

President Kennedy approves a new secret plan, Operation Mongoose, to overthrow Fidel Castro and his revolutionary government in Cuba

April 1962

U.S. Jupiter missiles become operational in Turkey

May 1962

Khrushchev authorizes Soviet military officials to place nuclear missiles in Cuba

August 1962

After receiving reports of Soviet missiles and nuclear bombers in Cuba, Kennedy approves U-2 surveillance flights over the island

September 1962

In separate public statements on September 4 and 13, Kennedy warns against Soviet missiles or offensive weapons in Cuba

Sunday, October 14, 1962

A U-2 spy plane takes photos of Soviet missile sites in Cuba

Monday, October 15, 1962

Key members of the military and Kennedy's Cabinet are notified about the missiles

Tuesday, October 16, 1962

Kennedy gets news about the missiles in the morning and is meeting with advisers by noon

Wednesday, October 17, 1962

Another U-2 flight discovers even more dangerous missiles that are capable of hitting targets more than 2,200 miles (3,540 km) away

Thursday, October 18, 1962

President Kennedy meets at the White House with Soviet Foreign Minister Gromyko, who tells him there are no offensive Soviet weapons in Cuba

Friday, October 19, 1962

Kennedy travels to the Midwest to continue his campaign schedule

Saturday, October 20, 1962

When Kennedy returns to Washington, D.C., some members of EXCOMM recommend a blockade of Cuba, but other advisers want to take stronger action

Sunday, October 21, 1962

Kennedy makes his decision and orders a blockade of Cuba; he requests airtime from all television networks for Monday night

Monday, October 22, 1962

Kennedy informs Congress of the blockade and gives a televised speech to the American people

Tuesday, October 23, 1962

The United States and the world react to the news of the crisis; debate begins at the United Nations; Kennedy signs an official proclamation putting the quarantine into effect the following day

87

Timeline

Wednesday, October 24, 1962

The U.S. quarantine goes into effect at 10 A.M.; several Soviet ships stop or turn around rather than cross the quarantine line

Thursday, October 25, 1962

A dramatic showdown occurs at the U.N. Security Council between U.S. Ambassador Adlai Stevenson and Soviet Ambassador Valerian Zorin; Kennedy responds to a letter from Khrushchev, saying the only way out of the crisis is to remove the missiles

Friday, October 26, 1962

The first ship is stopped as part of quarantine and allowed to continue after being inspected; Khrushchev sends a letter to Kennedy saying he will remove missiles if the United States promises to not invade Cuba

Saturday, October 27, 1962

A U-2 spy plane flown by Major Rudolf Anderson is shot down over Cuba; a second letter from Khrushchev seems to take a step back from his earlier letter

Sunday, October 28

The crisis comes to an end as Khrushchev announces on official Soviet radio that the missiles will be removed from Cuba

November 20, 1962

The United States lifts its blockade of Cuba after the missiles are removed

August 5, 1963

The United States and the Soviet Union sign the Limited Test Ban Treaty, which bans atmospheric (above ground) nuclear arms tests; the treaty lays the groundwork for the Anti-Ballistic Missile (ABM) Treaty in 1972

November 22, 1963

President Kennedy is assassinated in Dallas, Texas

November 1989

The Berlin Wall comes down; this event, along with the collapse of the Soviet Union in 1991, represents the end of the Cold War

January 1999

Fidel Castro celebrates the 40th anniversary of coming to power in Cuba

88

On the Web

For more information on *The Cuban Missile Crisis*, use FactHound.

1 Go to *www.facthound.com*

2 Type in a search word related to this book or this book ID: 0756516242

3 Click on the *Fetch It* button. FactHound will find Web sites related to this book.

Historic Sites

John Fitzgerald Kennedy Library and Museum
Columbia Point
Boston, MA 02125
866/JFK-1960

Visitors can view exhibits about President Kennedy and see personal records and belongings.

National Museum of the U.S. Air Force
1100 Spaatz St.
Wright-Patterson AFB, OH 45433
937/255-3286

Visitors can view more than 300 aircraft and missiles and learn about the history of the U.S. Air Force.

Look for all the Books in this Series

The Cuban Missile Crisis:
To the Brink of War
ISBN 0-7565-1624-2

Hiroshima and Nagasaki:
Fire from the Sky
ISBN 0-7565-1621-8

The Korean War:
America's Forgotten War
ISBN 0-7565-1625-0

Pearl Harbor:
Day of Infamy
ISBN 0-7565-1622-6

September 11:
Attack on America
ISBN 0-7565-1620-X

The Tet Offensive:
Turning Point of the Vietnam War
ISBN 0-7565-1623-4

Glossary

ambassador
a government official who represents his or her country in a foreign country

attorney general
the head of the U.S. Justice Department

ballistic missile
a missile lifted high into the atmosphere by a rocket engine. The missile then falls toward a target through gravity.

Cabinet
a president's group of advisers who are heads of government agencies

communism
a political system in which there is no private property and everything is owned and shared in common

DEFCON (defense condition)
the five levels of alert for U.S. military and nuclear forces, from DEFCON 5 in peacetime up to DEFCON 1 in war

dictator
a person who rules with complete authority, without political opposition or limits of power

hydrogen bomb
the most destructive weapon ever created. It uses the power of nuclear fusion to create massive destruction.

ideology
a system of ideas and beliefs held by individuals or groups, often used to refer to the ideas that form the basis of a political movement

imperialism
the policy of one country imposing its rule over another country, usually to promote political or economic interests

mobilization
getting troops and weapons ready for battle and putting forces in place to do battle

NATO (North Atlantic Treaty Organization)
the alliance between the United States, Canada, and Western European nations formed after World War II

offensive weapons
military weapons used to attack an enemy (as opposed to defensive weapons, which are meant only to defend against an enemy's attack)

quarantine
the practice of isolating a person, place, or thing; usually used to stop the spread of disease. In the Cuban Missile Crisis, the term was used instead of *blockade*, which is considered an act of war.

surface-to-air missile (SAM)
ground-based missile fired at targets in the air, used to shoot down aircraft

secretary
the head of a government department

status quo
existing state of affairs

Strategic Air Command (SAC)
part of U.S. Air Force that controls nuclear bomber fleet

SOURCE NOTES

Chapter 1

Page 15, line 8: Kennedy, John F. Public speech. 4 Sept. 1962.

Chapter 2

Page 21, line 3: PBS American Experience.
http://www.pbs.org/wgbh/amex/castro/filmmore/pt.html

Chapter 3

Page 33, line 9: Ernest R. May, ed., and Philip D. Zelikow. *The Kennedy Tapes: Inside the White House During the Cuban Missile Crisis*. Cambridge, Mass.: The Belknap Press of Harvard University Press, 1997, p. 115.

Page 34, line 2: Ibid., p. 149.

Page 35, line 3: Ibid., p. 149.

Page 35, line 6: Ibid., pp. 96, 166.

Page 35, line 14: Ibid., p. 159.

Page 37, line 2: Ibid., p. 169.

Page 37, line 8: Ibid., p. 169.

Chapter 4

Page 40, line 22: *The Kennedy Tapes: Inside the White House During the Cuban Missile Crisis*, p. 182.

Page 40, line 24: Ibid.

Page 40, line 26: Ibid.

Page 42, line 25: James N. Giglio. *The Presidency of John F. Kennedy*. Lawrence, Kan.: University Press of Kansas, 1992, p. 196.

Page 44, line 18: Ibid., p. 204.

Page 45, line 6: John F. Kennedy. Public Speech. 22 Oct. 1962.

Page 46, lines 1–10: Ibid.

Page 47, lines 1–19: Ibid.

SOURCE NOTES

Chapter 5

Page 54, line 12: Elie Abel. *The Missile Crisis*. Philadelphia, Pa.: Lippincott, 1966, p. 121.

Page 54, line 24: Ibid.

Page 54, line 26: Ibid.

Page 55, line 3: Ibid.

Page 57, line 3: Ibid.

Chapter 6

Page 62, sidebar: Robert F. Kennedy. *Thirteen Days: A Memoir of the Cuban Missile Crisis*. New York: W.W. Norton, 1969, p. 73.

Page 63, line 9: *The Missile Crisis*, p. 153.

Chapter 7

Page 71, lines 1–4, 7–19: BBC News Talking Points. <http://news.bbc.co.uk/1/hi/world/americas/2317931.stm>

Chapter 8

Page 75, line 5: *Thirteen Days: A Memoir of the Cuban Missile Crisis*. New York: W.W. Norton, 1969, p. 81.

Page 77, line 22: A.V. Fursenko. *One Hell of a Gamble: Khrushchev, Castro, and Kennedy, 1958–1964*. New York: W.W. Norton, 1997, p. 284.

Page 77, line 27: Ibid., p. 285.

Page 79, line 11: *The Fog of War*. Dir. Errol Morris. Sony Pictures Classics, 2004.

SELECT BIBLIOGRAPHY

Abel, Elie. *The Missile Crisis.* Philadelphia, Pa.: Lippincott, 1966.

Fursenko, A.V. *One Hell of a Gamble: Khrushchev, Castro, and Kennedy, 1958–1964.* New York: W.W. Norton, 1997.

Giglio, James N. *The Presidency of John F. Kennedy.* Lawrence, Kan.: University Press of Kansas, 1992.

Kennedy, Robert F. *Thirteen Days: A Memoir of the Cuban Missile Crisis.* New York: W.W. Norton, 1969.

May, Ernest R., ed., and Philip D. Zelikow. *The Kennedy Tapes: Inside the White House During the Cuban Missile Crisis.* Cambridge, Mass.: The Belknap Press of Harvard University Press, 1997.

Perez, Louis A., Jr. *Cuba and the United States.* Athens, Ga.: University of Georgia Press, 1997.

Thompson, Robert Smith. *The Missiles of October: The Declassified Story of John F. Kennedy and the Cuban Missile Crisis.* New York: Simon & Schuster, 1992.

FURTHER READING

Brubaker, Paul. *The Cuban Missile Crisis in American History.* Berkeley Heights, N.J.: Enslow Publishers, 2001.

Carter, E.J. *The Cuban Missile Crisis.* Chicago: Heinemann Library, 2003.

Chrisp, Peter. *The Cuban Missile Crisis.* New York: World Almanac Library, 2001.

Index

ABOUT THE AUTHOR

Paul J. Byrne is a writer and editor from Connecticut. He holds a degree in history and economics. Paul writes about people, history, and the natural world and has worked on a number of children's publications. He lives with his wife, Marina, and daughter, Stella, in Norwalk, Connecticut.

IMAGE CREDITS